# Get a Real Job

## Memoirs, Stories, Tips & Crude Talk With a Semi Sober Waiter

By
FRED JOSEPH

FRED JOSEPH

Get a Real Job

Copyright © 2019 Fred Joseph
All rights reserved.

This book is protected under the copyright laws of the United States of America. No part of this document may be reproduced or transmitted in any form or by any means, electronic, mechanical, photocopying, recording, or otherwise, without prior written permission of Fred Joseph.

Written request for reprint or other permissions should be communicated through email: FredJLive@gmail.com

ISBN: 978-0-578-57173-7

# About The Author

Fred Joseph is a slightly above-average guy who spends his free time in the creative world but has had many jobs in the world of industry, particularly in the hospitality industry. Those practical jobs have spanned over 7 years and many types of establishments, ranging from dive bars to elite country clubs.

## GET A REAL JOB

He wants it to go on the record that this is his first book, but not his last, and that he prefers crunchy peanut butter over creamy. He has had many customers and experiences that have either rubbed him the wrong way or left a great impression, giving him the itch to write about this industry that he loves to hate… or is it hates to love?

## TABLE OF CONTENTS

| | |
|---|---|
| **ABOUT THE AUTHOR** | **2** |
| **INTRODUCTION (A LITTLE HEADS-UP TO YOU)** | **1** |
| **CHAPTER 1** | **5** |
| **MY JOURNEY PART 1: LOSING MY VIRGINITY** | **5** |
| **CHAPTER 2** | **13** |
| **MY JOURNEY PART 2: A WHOLE NEW WORLD** | **13** |
| **CHAPTER 3** | **21** |
| **MY JOURNEY PART 3: LEVEL UP, LEVEL UP** | **21** |
| **CHAPTER 4** | **27** |
| **CHAPTER 5** | **41** |
| **MY JOURNEY PART 4: MORE FLASHY AND MORE EXTRAVAGANT!** | **41** |
| **CHAPTER 6** | **49** |
| **MY JOURNEY PART 5: STEPPING UP MY BOUJEENESS** | **49** |
| **CHAPTER 7** | **59** |
| **MY JOURNEY PART 6: FLY HIGH OR CRASH AND BURN?** | **59** |
| **CHAPTER 8** | **65** |
| **CHAPTER 9** | **77** |
| **MY JOURNEY PART 7: KING OF NY (NOT REALLY)** | **77** |
| **CHAPTER 10** | **85** |
| **STORY PART 8: FAMILIAR TERRITORY** | **85** |

**CHAPTER 11**                                **91**
**MY JOURNEY PART 9: CHECK, PLEASE!**  **92**
**ACKNOWLEDGMENTS**                  **95**

FRED JOSEPH

# INTRODUCTION (A LITTLE HEADS-UP TO YOU)

Um, let's see... so this is the part where I introduce myself and explain the reasons I wrote this book. I think it's supposed to give you a glimpse into my soul and reveal my inspiration. Oooh, so exciting!

But first, thanks for buying (or bootlegging) this masterpiece. I really appreciate the support and hope you enjoy the craziness that's been what seems like 20 years(less than 10 years) of my life. As a matter of fact at the beginning of this book writing, I was still working in the industry as a Server/Bartender. My time in the industry is coming to an end soon, so I thought what better time than now to share my experiences and perspectives.

I feel like it's imperative that you know no idiots were harmed during the writing of this book, though some may have been during the experiences contained within (but don't worry, not physically..I think).

I curated (I like that word... and parentheses) a special playlist to get me in the creative zone and then I just let it flow all freestyle-like, going off the top of my head. I wanted to write about it in a slightly unorthodox way. I envision us talking and laughing at all these stories of customers & workers, the good and the bad (mostly bad), and taking shots in memory of my co-workers who were in the crumb-ridden trenches with me.

So this book isn't meant to birth any grammarian. This book ain't gonna be perfect and what do you care anyway? I nor do I aim to win a Pulitzer Prize so just shut off that part of your brain and enjoy your beer(or skinny ice double mocha frappuccino chai tea soy latte with whip cream cinnamon) and my insight.

Don't get offended if I, the voice in your head reading this book to you, complain about or make fun of your "type" during this book, as in the type of customer you are. I mean, we're still besties and all that good shit so don't take what is said personally (unless you're one of those type that get an orgasm from being offended then I got you covered ). I've also changed and left out names of certain places to protect privacy and feelings. This is all written in good spirits and is meant to be simple, raw (not as much as I would like thanks editor), and fun. If inappropriate language or being curt of politically incorrect offends you, then you might want to stop reading now. Most people in my industry talk like sailors, swearing left and right, and I'm no damn different. But no, seriously, pick the book (or ebook) back up and relax. For the most part, I'm writing this in a tongue in cheek sort of way that I hope both service workers and customers alike will learn something and get a kick out of.

I will talk about some of the ins-and-outs of the

hospitality industry and though that encompasses bartenders, servers, busboys, valet, strippers, hosts, managers, bouncers, salesmen, cashiers, and blah blah you get the point, I am going to focus mainly on the tipped food and beverage sector, particularly the servers and bartenders. Why, you may ask? Well, it's because I can talk more of my shit with that since I've worked those two positions the longest. For you civilians, I have also thrown in things that we in the industry have recognized and would like to address. I even interviewed past coworkers and sprinkled in their quotes throughout this book. I also have a lot of inner thought (did I mention I like parentheses) and tend to go on tangents.

This was something I wanted to do even if I was new to it. I wrote this because I know there's a lot of people in this industry who can relate to what I've been or am currently going through. I also wrote this book because I thought it would be interesting to give outsiders a look at the "biz" from the perspective of those who work inside the industry. I've been in this service world for almost a decade (damn) and I feel like we in the industry are misrepresented or, more accurate to say, underrepresented.

I am a guy with a vast amount of interests and involved in a few other projects. I hated the idea of being boxed into a category that society (don't get me started on that) and people want to put you in. I want to better represent our world and to talk about certain things that we encounter with the customers, how I started, some stories over the years and how I overcame a crack addiction. I'm kidding...still smoking it. (Seriously, I'm joking). Email me for the REAL non-political reason why.

Alright, that's enough of the free bread. Let's dig in.

# Chapter 1

## My Journey Part 1: Losing My Virginity

I first got into this industry at the tender age of 19. I was young, tall and full of cum (I think that's how the saying goes). I was approached by a middle-aged (at the time) brunette lady with a Southern accent and she got me in the male escort business. I became a full-time gigolo out on South Beach catering to the more mature ladies, wearing my pin-stripe suits with suede briefs underneath (I only do suede in the winters. Standards, folks, standards. Plus, I have sensitive skin).

She was basically my pimp but more upscale-like. I prefer to say adult relations management. The split was 70/30 for me and the money wasn't too bad. Young Freddy Fred just slinging woo— Okay, okay, I'm joking! None of that Gigolo stuff happened but damn, wouldn't that make my bar stories even *more* interesting?

Alright, I'll quit messing around and tell you the real, less interesting way I got into this industry. Nothing else that happened outside of that at the time during those jobs. I'm saving those part of my life for the biography book OR a Rise and Fall TV special on me

(E! Hollywood what's up?).

So I was working at a big sports TV station covering the play-by-play data entry for basketball. Same company on channel 4 if you live in South Florida. Trust me it's not as sophisticated or glamorous as it sounds. It was actually an entry-level job and I think the only requirement was basic, competent sport knowledge. It was an easy and chill position, but the pay was low and only seasonal hours (very seasonal for me since I only covered the basketball season). After 3 years, I got tired of the small, inconsistent paycheck and decided to up my own game.

But what to do next? Well, 9-5 jobs weren't an option. I loathe the monotony and listening to the boss hold meeting after meeting about the same shit that won't be implemented by anyone, including themselves. No matter how hard you work, that bum coworker who doesn't do nothing will be getting the same salary as me. That right there probably annoyed me the most and is what inevitably tipped the scale for me to quit every last 9-5 job I've ever had. My personal best record is quitting after 2 hours on the job. No disrespect (or maybe if you feel like it go ahead, let's argue I'm off today) to those that can do it, I can't. It bores the hell out of me.

I learned that some bartenders only work weekends yet still make the same as a 9-5 hellhole salary. And it looked so cool from the outside, I was intrigued. Pour a drink, make money and flirt with girls. Sold! Oh, Young Fred. The problem is, I didn't even drink then (I was a late bloomer... for a few other things as well), even though I was 21 or 22 at the time. I didn't know the difference between a gin or vodka, couldn't name more than two vodkas, only knew cheap beer brands from commercials or parties and WTF was a Manhattan? A borough in NYC, duh. No? I didn't know pour counts, the lingo, etc. You get it.

The next logical step for Young Fred to take was to go to bartending school for two weeks. So fast forward two weeks, a 1-night encounter (My bad, I lost your #), my whole monthly budget gone and feeling like I finish my bachelor degree, I graduated. It was time for Young Fred to get out there and tackle the imbibed world of bars with his newly printed bartending certificate.

Yay, right? Nay.

Apparently, that pricey and hard-earned piece of paper meant shit at the bars and restaurants. One manager even laughed at me when I presented it to him at an interview. It turns out that in this industry, experience is king. They don't care about no certificate without the experience. After all, anyone can memorize a couple of drinks but the ability to actually work behind a bar is waaaay different.

People come at with you with different drink orders, you got to know who came first, what drinks were ordered, line them up in the most efficient way to knock them out, memorize prices, track payments and which tabs are opened or closed, etc. etc. Yeah, it's definitely a different animal, NOT that I knew any of that shit at the time. I just thought those managers were assholes who passed up on a great employee (still do, a little).

Young Fred, meet Catch 22. You can only get

hired if you have experience but how do you get experience if no one will hire you? Sound familiar? I'm sure you can relate and I plan to go on a rampage about the absurdity of it in another book, but I'll stay focused on Young Fred's plight. What did this crafty little SOB do to get his foot in the door?

Well, he kicked that shit open.

I put down bars and restaurants that were closed down for good on my resume and prepped a few friends to act as former managers. How would they prove I didn't work there? What did I have to lose if they did? And besides, I *did* actually know more of the basics of bartending then someone just walking in off the street. I *did* actually learn stuff at the bartending school. I wasn't worried about being put on the spot because I'm pretty composed in these situation as a person—especially since I could back up my shit if tested behind the bar. Worst case scenario is that they shoot me and I dead, probably just get fired.

So, here you go, Mr. Manager. Here is my web of ssttrettcchhed truth that I will slowly untangle as I get REAL experience.

Even with my exaggerated resume, I heard the same old recycled manuscript from hiring managers for weeks. "We're interviewing a couple people today and will get back to you by tomorrow" aka "Fuck outta here". We ain't hiring you but we ain't telling you to your face so you don't snap on us".

I finally did get hired at a Peruvian/Italian restaurant as a bartender. I may have been brand new but I knew what I was doing (mostly) and that place was also brand newish (Google isn't clear if that is a real word or not, but I like it so I don't care), so I felt it was a win-win for both parties. It was my first real hospitality job offer and I didn't have any preconceived notion of what type of place I would like to work at or what made the most money.

Plus, I would get free food, so I was sold. As usual, I said fuck it and just went with it.

Now, I'm not actually recommending anyone do what I did (I don't really care if you do but make sure you can back up your abilities that you claimed in the interview), and I've learned that there is actually a pretty sure-fire way to get your foot in the door without exaggerating your experience: catering.

Most catering jobs hire with little to no experience. As long as you understand the basics and have a nice personality, they're much easier to get. You don't handle much cash, if any, and a lot of time when you're doing an event, you are making a basic drink that even your idiot cousin can't screw up, like rum and coke, pouring wine, and what not. So there is always that higher road you can take.

### Normal Operating Hours, What Are Those?

This industry doesn't really operate like a 9 to 5 job for the most part. Most "real" jobs are Monday to Friday. Yay Friday! Oh Goodies! Well, in our industry that's normally when the party is just getting started. And by party, I mean work. If anything it might be the antithesis of 9-5's, our jobs are actually designed to cater to those who work 9 to 5 so we are busiest during their breaks and time off mainly. It's no surprise then that most bar and club workers live the vampire life, working all night and sleeping during the day.

Good luck dating or having a social life with one of us, you Day-walkers.

Set days & times to work is a foreign concept to most of us. Closing time does not equal clocking out time, especially for bars and clubs. Restaurants and hotels tend to have more reasonable hours, but still not 9 to 5, which may be better or worse depending on who you are. Look, I don't want to get into all the different types of establishment—not enough in the budget to get too much into it—ask Siri or something. I've been mostly a waiter and bartender but I've worked damn near every position and establishments in the beginning. I've worked in restaurants, hookah bars, nightclubs, private clubs, catering, hotels, you name it (except the strip clubs, not for a lack of trying though).

I've seen some things. It takes a certain type person to work in the industry. But no matter what the position, you can expect an ever changing, non-traditional schedule.

### Moment with a F&B battle-tested vet:

**Kevon/Server, NY**


**Best way to describe the industry?**

The hospitality industry is like a huge butt on steroids

that you kiss every day. You get so addicted to the fast cash that you don't even realize that you are walking all over your own pride just doing it.

**Things you wish customer would know?**

How to use their common sense and be realistic.

**Best and worst thing about the industry?**

The best things about the industry is the quick cash and once in a while, you will meet some amazing people. The worst thing is that it makes you realize how nasty, disgusting and selfish human beings really are.

# Chapter 2

## My Journey Part 2: A Whole New World

Let's fast forward a few months and a fling later.

I was looking for something better now that I had picked up some useful skills and actual experience at the restaurant. The folks there were cool but they weren't the most organized or the busiest since their business was new itself. Half the time, the customers were related to the owners and weren't exactly paying for anything. I liked them but I had bills (or at least what I considered bills at the time, oh, Young Naïve Fred). I needed something more fast-paced so I turned my sights to the busy metropolitan cities and zoomed in on South Beach. It wasn't long before I got my chance.

I saw an ad on event gig section of Craigslist. They needed a barback in South Beach for *that night*. A barback is basically what a busboy is to a server. They set up the bar, stock and help the bartender throughout the shift. They help with refilling, discarding things and whatever else needs attention, including security at times.

A good barback and busser is the backbone of an establishment. They don't get enough credit, without them certain places would crumble. Shout out to you all. Also, keep in mind the bartenders and servers have to tip them out of out of their own tips, so just remember the next time you want to be a cheap fucker. Alright, I'm calm, I got a coffee in hand and everything is all good.

My point is, a barback's job isn't as glamorous as a bartender's, but it is a good way to get your foot in the door and that's exactly what I was trying to do.

A word of caution, though: good barbacks are hard to find or replace, so many places would rather keep you in that position if the bar's running smoothly than give you a promotion, even way past your due time.

My advice? Be an underachiever. Get the job done: no more, no less. Don't slack but just be good, not great, if your goal is to be a bartender (I'm such a great motivational speaker, aren't I?). And watch closely to what the bartender is doing and learn to ask questions. Think of yourself as the bartender's apprentice.

Anyway, back to my story. I applied and got called into work that night. At the time, I was living in the next county over (Park East, what up! If you know, you know) and I didn't have a car yet. One of my right-hands, Jay, would drive me to interviews and other jobs, as well as most of our adventures and escapades.

That night, Jay drove me to South Beach and maaaan, was that an experience! South Beach was a different beast (back then, not the current boring South Beach) and just driving through the streets and past the crowds got your blood pumping. There were all types of people, eccentric, straight, gay, lesbian, Russian, Cuban, Haitian, club promoters, old money, new money, hustlers (male and females). I mean everything. Ferraris, Jag's, Hummers etc. everywhere. Food was an option at 4 in the morning (mostly pizza but isn't that the only food that matter at 4am?) That part remained me of NYC. People were flashy and bright, very bright as a matter of fact… too bright with all these damn colorful clothes.

Neon this. Neon that. I wonder if that's the reason why everyone has shades on day and night… hmm…

The job was at a hookah bar and as soon as I walked in, I could feel the excitement. The crowd was different than the Peruvian restaurant, more diverse and upbeat. The place stayed open longer than even I was accustomed to and there was more money flowing around than I had ever seen at the time. Young Fred was excited. I made more money that night than the last two weeks at the old job and got hired permanently (why wouldn't they hire me?). I blew all the money that night on bad cocaine and cheap hookers and woke up in a strange hotel with a tattoo and I am definitely lying again about the last sentence. Would've been another great bar story but better yet, I got my foot in the South Beach door.

I made a lot of money and had fun doing it. I wasn't leaving. Yet.

### Hourly Wages?

Let's talk about a little thing called money. For the most part, people in this industry work on tips/gratuity and get minimum wages (sometimes even less than that). A lot of 9-5ers assume we're getting standard wages *plus* tips, but that's just not the case. There are other 9-5ers that know our hourly wage is well-below par, but don't care. There is a standard tipping percentage between 15-20% for the most part, or more if the service was exceptional, and some would say 18-22%. That plus our hourly wage sounds like it would add up to a lot of money, right?

Well, some bartenders and waiters get paid as low as $2.13/hour (New Jersey, we feel you), but the normal hourly wage is only $5.50-$7.50. Needless to say, we really do rely greatly on tips. There are a lot of cheap people who don't tip (usually the most demanding one) or don't look at the job as an actual job. I'm talking about paying-for-college, single mothers, and harder-working-than-you type of servers that rely on these tips. How busy a place is fluctuates like crazy (bad weather, off-season, new place opened, etc.) so it's not an accurate thing for you to try to calculate how much money we make when we are the ones dealing with inconsistent and unpredictable incomes.

Some of you may ask why you have to tip for good service. Well, because you knowingly decided to walk your cheap-ass into a SERVICE-BASED tip establishment. You could've easily picked up a sub at Publix (what some of you know about Publix?) or driven through a fast-food joint and not be expected to pay a tip. Our tips are *part of* our income, not a bonus.

For you jackoffs (I never use that word in person but I'm really liking it now) that like to say "if you don't like it, go work in another industry"—first off, go fuck yourself (respectfully, of course) and second, the next time you're bitching about your hourly wage at your job, go work in a different industry.

Whew, that felt good.

Don't justify your terrible lack of character by telling people they must be in the wrong profession. You don't understand how our job works. Imagine if your employer decided to cut portion off your salary or hourly whenever they feel like it. Our tip should not depend on what's going on in your life, or how you're feeling, or if your sports team is losing (a real excuse I've been given). Granted, there are bartenders and servers who think they're entitled to a tip no matter the service they provide or even type-cast customers as non-tippers and approach the customer with a "I'm not getting tipped anyway" mindset (which is wrong, but based in reality. Yes, it's true. What the hell do you know!?). Those types of servers/bartender usually don't last and I get it if you don't tip based on their unusually bad service, but the vast majority of servers are trying to provide good service and should be paid what they're due.

Remember, tips are *part of* our income, not a bonus. Wendy can easily cater to you with your food coming out very quick and cheap. And guess what, you don't have to tip 1 cent!

Now that's not say that we are poor (well, not every one of us) and to donate to "Wehaventmadeshitfromourshifttoday foundation". That's silly....here's the real donation site, it's: Theimstillbrok— just playing. There are quite a few places where a waiter and bartender can make $300 plus a night, easily. Some places you can make as much as a doctors, or so I've heard. But regardless, every waiter and bartender has to work dollar for dollar, unlike a guaranteed salary whether you're slacking off or not. You might go to those high-priced places and think that you don't have to pay as high of a tip percentage because the bill is so much more, but that's just not how it works. That's why tips are percentage based, after all, not set values. We're not asking for anything extra (well I wouldn't mind...nevermind) just tip based on the service. Go ahead and tip them accordingly, it's okay. You'll be okay.

### Fred *Fantastic* Flashback: The Lonely Drunk Lady

Alcohol is cool and all. You know, it helps especially when you're trying to unwind and have a good time (shit, I know it helps me). BUT like with most things in life, too much of anything can be a negative (except coffee, I mean c'mon?!). So, at this one particular job, I was usually the first on the frontline when things happened.

Broken glass? me (Fuck you guys).

Fight? me (seriously you paid $20 to fight in a club in your best outfit?)

Annnd of course, drunk people? me!

So this one time we were trying to close up the club to go home but there was this lady who was drunk as hell. I wasn't sure if her friends were looking out for her or not and I think they may have even left her. I tried offering her water and we tried to get her up to put her in a taxi. One of the bouncers and I lifted her up by an arm on each side. As we started to move her closer to the door while the cab was on the way, she ends up throwing up all over my shoes and pants. I was wearing all black.

I dropped her arm off me as a natural reaction and the momentum from that made her fall on the security guard. They both fell and he was covered in vomit—and pissed off! I didn't care. I was so annoyed and grossed out, I just walked away.

From that point on, I never attempted to pick up or help another drunk person again at work. I'll leave that to the bouncers. Folks, two things. First: Know your limit. Second: If you're like, "Fuck that!" Cool, just make sure you go out with people who are your actual friends. I can't tell you how many times I've seen so-called friends leave a guy or girl alone by themselves, without their wallet and phone.

The abandoned friend comes back after sobering up the next day, asking questions like a Law and Order episode. I ain't seen or know nothing, sir or ma'am.

# Chapter 3

## My Journey Part 3: Level Up, Level Up

After working at the hookah bar for a few weeks, I wanted to move up from barback/busser/whatever they needed—you know, those owners who try to squeeze an extra position out of you, like server/mail carrier or busser/accountant. With the same pay, of course.

I wish Older Fred could've given me the same advice he gave you about doing your job and nothing more if you didn't want to get walked all over as a barback. I was even filling the role of a janitor and ladies, I love you all, but your bathroom was usually the messiest. Hugs and kisses though. I was beginning to discover some of the con's of the industry. Noticing a lot of annoying behavior and traits some of the customers had. But little did I knew that I was going to see those trait in every other place I was going to work at.

Some of them were leaving their drinks in the bathroom, friends who would or could not control their drunk friends, or girls grabbing me in the crowd…no wait, that part wasn't so bad. Never mind that.

I knew what type of money to be made (I was assuming at that point but wasn't too far off) and I was at the bottom. Young Fred pride wasn't going to be able to handle it for too long. The Fred now though wouldn't have minded (all lies). I didn't like doing those odds job while they were all these gorgeous women around and the pay wasn't as much as I should've been getting. Especially since I wasn't handling the money, the bartenders were. They tipped me out afterward. Didn't like that.

The worst part was being surrounded by all of these young, chic women with a job where I couldn't interact with them and instead was swabbing up spilled drinks and vomit in their presence. It was hurting my pride and squashing my mojo. It was time for me to level up.

Thankfully I got a job in no time at a big night club down the street. My timing couldn't have been better because shortly after leaving the hookah bar it was raided by the FBI.

Seriously. This isn't one of my "bar stories". There was a Russian mob ring there where they would disperse women to different hotels & lounge throughout South Beach and have them convince wealthy sucke-, I mean, men to come to the bar and get them so drunk they wouldn't realize how much money they were spending on bottles. The women would dump the drinks they had nearby and act like they were getting drunk too among other things.

Sounds crazy, but that was about on par for South Beach at the time. I would soon learn to not be surprised by anything down there.

The night club I went to work at was way more popular than the hookah bar and was along Washington Ave. between 8th and 9th Ave. I won't say the name of it, but it was probably one of the top 5 clubs (debatable) in South Beach in 2010. The concept to this day I haven't seen again. It was the only club doing that at least in Miami and New York City.

But this changed everything, the pace was faster and bigger. That shitty Jersey Shore show was filmed there (after I left, thaaaank you, universe), though I'm not sure if the name of the club was televised. I was still a barback runner, but it was different. I was dealing more with bottle service than the bar and was NOT doing all those other odd jobs. I would set up bottle service with the ice bucket, ice, napkins and all the chasers for more than 3 times the normal price in what is commonly considered the VIP section (Very Important People for my slow people. Just kidding, but not really. You should've known what it meant. Shame on you if you didn't).

This club's VIPs included celebrities every weekend. I met a few inside the owner's office and also helped prep bottle service for some. Some gained my respect and some lost it. Here's the lame part where I do some name dropping, I know, I know, but... yeah: Dennis Rodman (weird but very cool), Rick Ross, DJ Clue, Fat Joe (before the weight loss), Bobby Valentino (very short), DJ Envy, Jim Jones (Dipset days), Fonzworth Bentley (smooth-dancing, sharp-dressing mofo).There wasn't any one that had me starstruck and besides there is only three celebrities that could do that (no I'm not a groupie, shut up). Of course I'm not going to name them. With the added cost of the bottle service did come more privacy away from the main club crowd, aka us broke folks, so I was mainly on the dance floor, going back and forth from the bar. I took every opportunity to provide extra customer service to um... uh... certain customers. Life was great!

**Breaks & Eating**

Even though our industry is designed to feed and cater to guests on their breaks and time off, breaks and eating for employees is a funny concept in this industry. Some places (typically hotels or corporate places where the staff is getting a pooled or set hourly wage) have staff meals and even set time for breaks. For the rest of us, the only time we get to eat (officially) is before or after our shift. That means if you start at 4pm and get off at 4am (typical shift at one of my previous jobs), you don't get a meal for over 12 hours.

Can you imagine working at a high intensity job with little sustenance and be expected to have a smile on your face 100% of the time? Thankfully, with a little finesse and cooperation between coworkers, you can find ways to squeeze in bites and drinks (especially if our establishment serves food), but it can lead to all types of shitty eating and drinking habits.

## Moment with a F&B battle-tested vet:

**Jeff/Ex-Server, NY**

## How would you describe the industry?

The hospitality industry is one of the footholds of society because you can't replace great service, no matter what technology comes out. People literally go out to eat for the atmosphere and to be waited on. There's very few things that replaces a great venue, a dope dish and exceptional service.

## What you would like the customer to know?

I just really wish that customers would understand that the people serving them are human as well and that this is their job, just the same as someone going to work and sitting in a cubicle.

## The best and the worst part of the industry?

The best and worst part of the industry both reside in the same boat: the people you serve. Sometimes you will get that awesome person as a guest in your establishment that you can talk to about anything, they don't mind that you made one little mistake or even if you screw up, because they get that you are human. Then there is the opposite side of the same coin where you get the irrational guest that treats you as if you are a petty servant and as if you don't have an entire life outside of this job that THEY consider "menial". That's not how it works. We are both contributing members of the same society.

# Chapter 4

We're going to take a break here from my journey and focus on the customer, or rather, the customer types. For you civilians, this is the time to see if you are guilty of being one or more of these types and to promise to do better next time. For fellowmen, this is your chance to laugh and cry because you can relate to dealing with these people on a daily basis.

### Types of Customers We "Love" to Serve

Let's talk about the industry's "special" customers. The majority of us in this industry will provide the same great customer service regardless, but it's entertaining to poke fun at a customer, usually at their expense. Don't get your feelings hurt if you realize you're one of these customers. It's all in good fun.

1. **The demanding but cheap types:** this lovely customer is very demanding and picky. If there's a question to be asked, oh believe me, they'll ask it. They nitpick everything, EVERYTHING I said, damn it. They'll ask for recommendations and then order the opposite, complain about what they ordered or change the whole DNA makeup of what they

order into something completely different. Let's say Item #2 is a cheeseburger with wheat bun w/cheddar and fries. They'll ask for white bread instead, chicken patty instead of beef with swiss cheese which we don't carry and a bowl of cereal instead of fries. If the miracle happens where we made it possible, they'll say something like I don't like it (no shit) and want it comp. Oh yeah, and they tip terribly most of the time, if at all.

### Flashback

**Guest:** Do you know what particular cow milk was used for the cheese?

**Server:** Um—

**Guest:** Was it a grass fed cow or not? Also, what farm was it?

**Server:** (Inner voice: WTF is she talking about? She wanna order or not?) I'm not sure, I can ask. In the meantime, let me get everybody else's orders.

After getting everyone else's order and I'm about to leave to ask (I guess she kinda felt silly no one else was being difficult) she ordered a salad. COMPLETELY different items from her pop quiz option earlier. This happens way more than you think.

2. **The Outspoken type:** It's the guest in the

party who's not paying the bill but seems to have the most complaints and extra requirements. They even generously offer to complain for others who have no complaints (how thoughtful of them). This one will take the longest and will definitely have some expert tips about the food on the menu.

### **Flashback**
Me: How's everything?
Lisa: It's ok
The Outspoken One: No Lisa, give him the drink so he can make you another one
Lisa: It's fine
Me: What's wrong with it?
Lisa: It's fine-
The Outspoken One: You should give it to her for free, as a matter of fact
Me: ?!?!?!

3. **The "What's the cheapest thing on the menu?" types:** Ah, there's nothing like this question to start off with. This type is, well, self-explanatory and are the customer-type we don't expect to get any tips from. What's interesting, is these people are usually just cheap, not broke. I know one or two of them personally and I want to yell at them to go get a 2 for 1 burger deal at Burger King.

### **Flashback**

Me: Welcome to blah blah, sir. My name is Fred, I'll be your server today. Would you like som-

Guest: What's the cheapest thing on the menu?

Me: (inner voice: a happy meal at McDonalds two blocks a way) Side salad and fries?

Guest: Alright, can I get that with bread and do you charge for a refill?

Me: (Knew it) Yes, we do.

Guest: Extra bread, please.

Me: (sigh) Got you.

4. **The "We're not in a rush" types:** They're typically the person or group at the table that not all the members have arrived yet, who's telling you they are waiting on someone who is coming in a few (40) minutes while they hog the table. Or, they're the group who are having some kind of reunion or overdue night out. You come to check on them and they keep telling you "Oh, we haven't looked at the menu yet. Come back in a few minutes". After 3 trips of the same, you get hit with another large table(s) and then suddenly they are eager to order. Now they are definitely trying to get your attention.

You'll make them wait.

5. **The Separate Checks Type:** Splitting a

check and separating a check are two different things. Splitting it is straight down to equal shares and makes more sense but what do we know, we're just servers. The "separate" check types wants me to run individual checks for each person at the table, whether it's 2 or 30. There are times when this makes sense (business, just met, etc) but I'll never understand why family or "great" friends request them. Why not just go sit at different tables and wave and talk from there, if that's how you want me to treat the table? Depending on where I'm working, I don't entertain it. ESPECIALLY if it's busy. Pool all money together and pay.

I remember these women wanting to split a check of one fries order……..

### **Flashback**
Me: So it's 22 ppl here, right? How do you all want to pay?
Guests: Separate checks

Me: Everyone?

Guest: Yup, 22 separate checks, is that cool?

Me:………

Guest: Is that cool?

Me: Yup *jaws clench* (Server inner voice: Why the fuck are they eating together?)

Guest: Great.

Me: *Smiles* (Inner voice: Go fuck ya'llselves) *still smiles*

6. **The Expert type:** They seem to think they know a lot more than you about the menu and the restaurant you've been working at for years. They'll swear the bathroom used to be on the left 2 years ago or "what happened to that sushi option that you used to sell?" at a burger joint. Just on and on.

### **Flashback**

Me: Are you ready to order sir?

Guest: How come the price for a burger changed?

Me: ?

Guest: It used to be $5 now it's 8.

Me: Sir it's been $8 since we open the 3 weeks ago.

Guest: No, it was 5 when I came a few years ago.

Me: (Inner voice: so you want to order or

nnoo?) Damn, that's crazy.

Guest: Where's your manager?

Me: Be right back (Inner voice: Great! Now, I can go check on my other tables)

7. **The aware non-tipping type:** Die. Just kidding (am I, though?) Oh, and to the foreigners, cut that shit out. You know what U.S. tipping standards are.

8. **King and Queen Entitled:** Apparently, the rules don't apply to these folks. Section's closed? They insist on sitting there. We don't sell Coke, only Pepsi? What an outrage! They think the 5% tip they are going to leave comes with a side plate of disrespect. It almost seems like they get a kick out of going against every establishment policy. They also love pulling the "customer is always right" card and hate the word no.

### Flashback

Bartender: Sir sorry that's for bottle service only.

Guest: But there's no one there.

Bartender: I know but it's closed off for guests who get a bottle, I'm sorry.

Guest: Why can't we sit here? When someone comes we'll get up.

Bartender: I'm sorry, sir, you can't.

Guest: Is this how you treat your customers?

Bartender: (Inner: here we go again) Sorry.

Guest: I'm out, this place is bullshit.

Bartender: Sorry to hear that, enjoy your night.

Guest: Fuck off!

Bartender: (Inner voice: Haha) Take care.

9. **The lounging type:** They typically either order one drink at the bar and nurse it (usually during a sports time) or they'll order, eat, close their tabs and hang around for hours at the table. See here's the thing that people don't know (or maybe they do): Servers usually have sections. It means each server has a certain number of tables they have to make money from by serving customers and then flipping that table for the next customers.

When customers hog a table after they close out, the server can't sit nobody else aka they make less money. It's even worse when it's busy and other customer need to find a table because they haven't been served yet. Not saying you have to get the fuck up immediately but be reasonable. You can't go tell that one story you told a hundred times before outside?

10. **The waving the dollar around type:** This type is usually waving money at you or in your face during a packed bar. If this is you, LOOOK-AT-ME: YOU ARE ANNOYING. We already acknowledged you. Bartenders usually see everybody and the order of people who came first (well, most of us) and we have a shit-ton of drinks and tabs in our head that we are sorting out.

We will usually give you the same death stare my mom used to give me at church from across the room when I was young and acting out (I got chills just now).

Relax and think about why it wouldn't be smart to order a mojito at club with a packed bar. We will get to you. We wouldn't come to your job and wave money in your face while you're handling a task. You're not a 7-year-old.

11. **The Mr./Mrs. No taste bud type:** They always say "I don't taste any liquor in this drink". Ma'am/sir all pours are usually the same at an establishment but feel free to order a double (or I can give you an AA number). They swear we didn't pour any alcohol. Or the type that don't ever taste the so-called brand of mixer they requested when it's in their drink. We usually make the drink the same way and after we give them the "second" drink they go "well that's better". Alcoholic placebo effect, anyone? Shit one time I took the drink, made one lap around the bar counted for about 10 seconds and gave her the same drink, she told me "Now that's how it's supposed to taste".

By the way folks, the bartender and server don't make shit from trying to charge you more or pour less. We don't own the place, remember that, and aren't trying to cheat you.

12. **The "Trust me" type:** This type usually tries

to order for another person that most of the time are underaged and they tell you the person is legal "trust me". Um…no.

13. **The "I'm ready" type:** This one tries very hard to get your attention, urgently signaling that they are ready at the bar but when you get to them, they invite the rest of party to order while they decide (who by the way usually doesn't know what they want).

If this is you…just know you're slowing the whole bar down. Also the types at a table that tell us they are ready and then they are like "um… let's see uh…" I usually tell (not ask) them I'll be back at that point. Know what the hell you want if you're going to wave us down like you're catching the Holy Ghost at a TD Jakes church.

14. **The daycare parents type:** Ah, maaaan! Parents, we love you and all, but this is for the type that comes to restaurants letting the kids take all the sugar and dumping it all on the table or crayons on the table, thinking it's cute. That shit ain't cute. We got to clean it. Handle your kids. This ain't a daycare (Shameless plug

alert: Email me for a good one if you're in NYC). I've even seen this lady watch her baby playing with a steak knife, what's wrong with some of you?

**Fred *Fantastic* Flashback: Facades and Ego-Stroking**

People watching was becoming my new favorite thing in the industry. When you're working on the floor on a consistent basis and there is so much going on, your awareness level has to increase depending on how sharp you are. You pretty much know what's going on all around for the most part and there was a lot to notice about South Beach. South Beach is a big mirage where everyone's trying to appear a certain way. Guys rent luxury cars for the weekend but fronting like he owns it. Ladies live 3 to a bedroom, sharing clothes and coming to the club acting like they are rich models. These are all true things I knew about or saw personally.

One shift at the club, there was a gentleman that looked between 40-50 years old, having a bottle service by himself. There are usually groups of vultures— I mean opportunistic women—that tend to linger or "conveniently" be within the eye sight of those in the bottle service area. It was a common thing. So anyway, the guy invited two of the women over to the VIP section with him and another bottle was ordered. Lots of fake laughing and shoulder-rubbing going on. I looked again, there were two more girls and I saw one call another one over. I went there to replace the ice buckets and heard the cocktail waitress ask him if he was cool with all the girls there. He said it was cool, they can all chill with him. A lot of guy's egos on South Beach are easily stroked, which makes them easy to read. One of the girls said something, I think it was to order another bottle. Some of the other girls had also ordered shots among themselves. I mean all this alcohol around and everyone still looked thirsty.

The girls were sure helping themselves while the guy was feeling like the man in this biissshhh, but the vibe was weird. Some of the girls were giggling among themselves and had certain looks on their faces. A few hours later, the guy wanted to close out but he was saying he didn't order some of the things on the bill. We told him the girls in his party ordered them. He looked all annoyed but I guess he wanted to keep the front up (you know, the South Beach way) so he paid. I mean, 'why not?' he probably thought to himself, with all these women at his area SURELY he was going to take one home, right?

Well, he made the mistake of going to the bathroom or something and returned when I was helping my coworker clean the VIP area. He looked around in surprise and asked why we got rid of his bottles. We told him there was nothing left. All the women that were in his VIP section had drank his shit and left the club. Me and my coworker were trying to hold back our laugh. The look on his face was priceless, as if he poured a big bowl of cereal only to discover that someone left an empty milk carton in the fridge. He left the club alone and with pockets a few hundred dollars lighter. That was definitely the main topic discussed during our afterwork drink that night (morning).

Fellas, watch out for liquor hustlers. Don't let your ego cost you money that you may or may not have because we don't want to hear you argue about the bill and we're still going to get our gratuity no matter how much you fucked up.

To my lady hustlers, keep doing your thing. Especially if the guys want to keep up such facades in the clubs.

# Chapter 5

## My Journey Part 4: More flashy and more extravagant!

Not only was the money better at my new night club job, but I felt like I was getting paid to party. I was in my early 20s, getting a boost in money and was single-ish.

You may wonder, "Was Young Fred involved in all types of shenanigans and inappropriate activity?" Yoooouu fucking right he was!

It was South Beach, after all, where groups of female tourists flock from around the world. I got afterparty invites and went to their hotels or sometimes I would meet others more eager for attention *inside* the club. Working there, you tend to have a bit more access to quiet spots. You also get to know a lot of DJs, promoters, bouncers, owners and such who had access to other clubs and restaurants. I would get in free in a lot of different clubs and even got free drinks. I think my diet at that time consisted mainly of alcohol, pizza, red bull and coffee in no specific order.

There were a lot of days I'd only get 1-2 hours of sleep. I would die if I even considered doing that now, but yeah. I can only say so much about things I've done during that time for many different reasons but stay tuned later in life. Just know I got a lot of shit out of my system, take that how you want to. Because I wasn't driving, to get to work I would mostly catch a few bus to the next county to go to work and my boy would pick me up halfway between.

So with that being said they were some limit to my fun courtesy of the bus schedule at times-- but all that's boring let's back to the story.

It was nice to watch people come in and enjoy themselves. Girls dancing bare foot. I never understood certain group of guys tendency to want get on stage & dancing with 1980's female pop stars dance type moves. And of course, my favorite: the sloppy drunk, unchaperoned birthday girls wearing a sash, licking the side of people's faces and then trying to have a "logical" conversation with staff about why she should be able to dance on top of the bar, despite busting her ass 3 times already.

It was a fun time but, you know, I also got an outside perspective on how people act in a crowd. When you're not a part of them, you start to see patterns: same pickup lines by guys, same responses by girls, and the little actions that cause big fights. You start to catch on to the psychology of certain human behavior and how oblivious or unconcerned people can be when in a crowd, like, for example, when staff members are trying to pass through.

I had to make that trek through the oblivious/unconcerned crowd countless time when running bottle service and it usually went something like this:

> Me: Excuse me (as I'm carrying ice or a pack of beer)
>
> Guest: (not moving)
>
> Me: Excuse me! (getting annoyed because it's getting harder to hold)
>
> Guest: (not moving)

And then, I would do 1 of 3 things:

1. Yell EXCUSE ME! (at which point they get startled or give me a look, but they'll move)
2. Bump them with whatever I was carrying or wet them with ice "by accident", offering a "my bad" or give them that "oopsie" look, like, I told you to move.
3. I would put whatever I was carrying down on the floor in the middle of the crowd and go to the guy's face (never the ladies, I was too busy flirting with them. Don't judge me.) and tell him the shit that I'm carrying is heavy as shit and when I say excuse me, move the fuck out the way! True story.

I was definitely more aggressive back then but it was really only the jerk-offs that set me off. For the most part, I knew that they were high or drunk by a certain time and couldn't be held accountable for their Walking Dead-like antics. I don't smoke (to each their own) but it was crazy to see how many would be getting high in the crowd. I had fun watching the security try to figure out who it was. I tell you what, though, I learned that if I ever wanted to do any drugs, they aren't that hard to find. I was being offered shit left and right. Lines in the bathrooms, behind the bar, everywhere. That did also come with the "undercover" cops trying to set you up. Those that know, *knows* who the cop were. They were usually easy to spot, but perhaps not as easy when already drunk or high.

Or stupid.

It was an interesting time in my life and part of me was evolving. I was making a lot of "friends" at the time and also learning a lot about customer's funny habits and behaviors. The money could be inconsistent at times, but it was still good. When you go from getting hourly wages paid weekly/biweekly to getting cash tips every night you work, it's pretty addictive. A con is that I would be getting cash tips every night so I would be a little reckless with the spending because I always thought I could just go back the next day and easily recoup.

And you got a wad of cash in your pockets with all temptation of South Beach, tricky situation to be in. Something I eventually got a handle on. The problem is, the nightclub business is a flaky industry, especially in a place like South Beach. Here one year and gone the next. I've seen it happen a few times.

I had only been working there for a year or so when the place started to go on the decline. I can smell when the ship is going down, so I started looking for another job. That's another nugget of wisdom for you: always have two jobs in this industry. You never know when you may be out of job due to unavoidable circumstances or if you wanna go off on a rude customer (Ahh, therapy).

This place I was working at shut down three weeks after I left. I know what you're thinking....I must be an undercover agent who is brought in to take big illegal operation BUT my life is not THAT exciting. I won't put the owner's business specifics out there. The owners went back to Chicago, they were cool and I will always appreciate them for bringing me on board. But I was already on to bigger and better things. I was working at another place on Miami Beach, not to be confused with South Beach since that is only certain blocks on the Miami Beach tip, from about 1st St to a little past Lincoln Road.

This new place was a private club hotel on Collins Ave and past 30th but before 50th (good luck trying to figure that one out, Carmen Sandiego).

## A Peek Inside the Mind of a Bartender/Waiter

The inner workings of the mind of a bartender/server would be similar to that of someone cooking 4 dishes at the same time, making sure to regulate the heat, prep every dish, while holding a crying baby, switching phone calls with 3 people on the line, playing tic tac toe, while watching Oprah, and dodging country sized mosquitos, all the while with the expectation of performing at a highly successful rate hanging over your head. Oh, and don't forget that you're probably hungry. Seem exaggerated? Ask a server or bartender... I mean a good one, not one who asked you what type of tequila you'd like in your Old Fashion (Sorry, Kelly. Step it up!).

We have to keep watch of who sat down, how many adults, how many kids, take drinks, be mindful of allergies (like seafood at a seafood restaurant), the timing of courses, check in with "need anything?" regularly and more. And then, you get sat with a 20 top (people) and all of a sudden that "not in a rush table" needs to order now. We have this web of tasks that we have to navigate, all with a smile on our face and a laugh for your shitty jokes (ok, some of them were funny).

Most of us survive by creating a strong alter ego (the Hyde to our Jekyll or the Venom to our Eddie Brock). Here's an example: your servers name is Mike and his alter ego is called Evil Mike. Ok, maybe that's too extreme… perhaps Asshole Mike? Ok fine, we'll go with Brash Mike. So, Customer X asks Mike while holding his menu, "How much for your fish & chips?" and Mike responds "$10" with a smile. Brash Mike, however, replies "The price is right in front of you dumbass". Obviously there are special circumstances like bad eyesight or illiteracy (no judgment, seriously), but that is how most servers cope with the um… But for the most part, I believe the inner voice helps us cope and deal with mentally, the high-volume amount of stupidity output aim at us on a daily basis. Coping mechanism in place since we can't punch someone in the throat ("violence is wrong folks") it helps a little. Some servers do let Venom rear its ugly head every now and again and sometimes pass it off as sarcasm or a joke (and I find it extremely entertaining), but the alter ego is usually kept well-restrained.

Work one day in this industry, it's fun.

## Moment with a F&B battle-tested vet:
### Savannah/Server, NY

### How would you describe the industry?

The serving industry is super misunderstood. Being in the hospitality industry could be the best gig, if at the right place. People don't understand servers at all, especially if they have never been one themselves. Servers work a lot harder than just writing down an order and bringing that order to a table.

### Best and worst of it?

The best part of the industry is the fast money and connections that are to be made. You meet so many people from all over and building those connections can even take you to some new places you never expected to go.

Worst part about the industry is hands down the inconsiderate costumers you come across. The people who don't understand how they are not your only customers and demand your attention even when they see you're clearly helping another customer at the moment. Those people who make you run all over the place for them and barely leave you 15%. People who know they are being overbearing and annoying and laugh it off and continue to do so. People who complain about every little thing and take things out on the server when it is clearly beyond their control.

### Crazy, funniest, favorite or weirdest story/memory?

I would probably say having an actor from my favorite TV show become a regular and recognizing me the second time he came in. (Fred spoiler: It was Omari Hardwick)

### What do you wish people knew about the biz?

I wish the people who have the mentality "I don't have to tip my servers" would just stay home or make that statement upfront before receiving those services! They would see how different their service would be. People like that really have some nerve. Especially when people know how little servers make per hour and they still have the nerve to say "well, then get another job if you don't like it". I wish everyone had to be a server or bartender at least once in their life so they would understand.

# Chapter 6

## My Journey Part 5: Stepping Up My Boujeeness

Now I'm working at the private club hotel. Oh, by the way, I forgot to mention I got promoted to bartend at the nightclub before I left. Not that it mattered to the hotel, they wanted me to start as a barback but I'm going to fast forward all the way to when I became a bartender there because it makes me feel cooler.

This member-only club was interesting and way more upscale. I had to step my game up. The staff had to wear button-down shirts with ties, suspenders, slacks, black shoes and all that fancy shmancy stuff. Drinks had fresh ingredients, juices were freshly squeezed every morning, and the bar had crushed ice (crushed ice), coal fire pizza oven, and so on. A place you'd probably find SaltBae at, seasoning your food or something. The majority of the clientele were artists, singers, rappers, Hollywood actors and actresses, certain types of rich people, and wannabes. But mainly people in the creative field.

I can't go into too many details because of the nature of the club and people I know that still work there, but it's amazing what celebrities and some people do when they have certain privacy and only particular people are allowed in. There is no cell reception inside the club, no media or journalists are allowed in, and basically, no suit-types. I don't think social media was that big yet around that time, but whatever happened there, stayed there. This meant that I now worked with a mix of snobs and cool people, not to mention plenty of posers.

I had a guy sit at the bar acting like a big shot, ordering shots for girls and when the bill came, he pulled be to the side to ask if I could split the tab across 4 different credit cards, 1 of which got declined. True story.

So this new job clientele was members only but was somewhat of a clubhouse chain, which mean it had a few branch in certain different major city locations around the world as well as corporate. With corporate, it's more politics (as most of you already know) and the guest here at this upscale place have potential to be more snobby and entitled. The more elite customer base meant more money a lot of the times, but you kind of had to suck it up because they're often the type who were inclined to complain to the GM or owner with the usual "Do you know who I am?" kind of attitude. "Nope, don't care, but I do care if you tip me well, so how can I be of service to you?" was pretty much my attitude in return.

I always took care of my guests and the very few complaints I received were from unappeasable assholes. I messed up an occasional order, but who doesn't? And when I did own up to it. A lot of people are forgiving of honest mistakes but this crowd did include a lot of pretentious douche bags who treated all staff like servants. The money did help ease the offense and I could never say I was jealous of these rich guys (or gals) because I plan on being one of them someday if I'm not already by the publishing of this book…

Now, there's so much I wish could write on this book but I'm not the type—plus I think I signed some papers or something. I met some interesting celebrities though: Russell Simmons (man, he curses as much as I do. Cool dude.), Tom Cruise (very enthusiastic & generous. He once gave everybody working that day an undisclosed amount of tips), Scottie Pippen (very laid back and chill), LeBron James (I don't have to look up to at most people since I'm pretty tall myself) and more.

Some customers liked to have their ego stroked, others were prideful, while still others suffered from inferiority complexes, it was amazing. This place was definitely a different atmosphere than I was used to. I learned a lot on this job about high-class fine dining. Everything from the psyche of certain class of customers, it's funny because I believe most servers and bartenders that do this long enough could almost qualify as a psychiatrist (seriously). I mean not many people can read people like we can. Enough babbling, I'll save it for my counseling support group sessions. But yes, I learned to cater to a customer type that expected a high standard of service (and superb level of ass-kissing. Joking…sort of).

I learned a lot about mixology at this hotel before it began to be a "thing". Mixologists are a bit different than bartenders because mixology is more about the flair and the science. They're crafting to either follow a recipe to the tee or creating their own cocktails with precise measurements, fresh ingredients, and often use innovative ingredients that surprisingly complement each other to make a great cocktail. It's like art, at times. Also being good at improvising certain ingredients. Certain tools were utilized to prep the drinks and others: like a blowtorch (you would be surprised by uses of it).

Some argue that mixologists and bartenders are the same thing, but it's more like all mixologists are bartenders but not all bartenders are mixologists. See a bartender make drinks and provide great experience but a mixologist also creates original drinks. Although nowadays they both seem like the same shit. The great ones can taste a drink and deduce what was used to make it. Or they can find the missing ingredient in a cocktail with over 5 different things added to it that's not in your common cocktail but enough about that. I hated it, I prefer to bartend. I was the speedy bartending type. Mixologist was a little bit more about the quality, innovation, passion, creating and speed of it along with experience. These guys take this shit very serious and some of them are really amazing.

I just like to make my classic drinks, beer etc and engaging the customers (or not. Thank you loud speakers at the club). Customer love to try new drinks and I'm not going to lie, I enjoyed the reaction from customers when they get excited and compliment me on my drinks. My specialty was/is apple martini, mojitos, and margaritas specifically for the ladies (*wink*). By the way I notice customers have a habit of coming to the bar and calling out a random drink they saw online or TV that was created in a different state and expects you to know it. LOOK PEOPLE NO BARTENDER KNOWS EVERY DRINK. Not even that one drink that just came out yesterday. Some drinks are, made specifically for certain bars.

I also figured out a lot about what my strengths and weaknesses were. Ironically, my style behind the bar was different then it was in my real life. I'm very systematic and borderline OCD when I work. I'm surgical with that shit. I liked to be efficient and precise, which actually stemmed from my laziness and effortless underachieving ways. I was determined to find the smartest way of doing things to save me as much time and effort possible. I would reset everything to how it was originally set. That meant that if there were two shakers next to a jigger, then that's how they should be placed after they've been used. My reasoning behind this madness was that if I got hit with a big crowd rush, I should be able to work blindfolded, knowing where to reach what I needed. I didn't want to go looking for something I needed every time I needed it, especially when there are 50 thirsty people in front of me. Otherwise, it would be like going into the battlefield and someone keeps moving your weapon. It did make it difficult to work with certain coworkers but it kept me in my groove.

I had second job (of course) at an airport while working at this hotel. So fast forward a few TMZ-worthy moments, a few respect-losing incidences with certain celebrities, and a few liver-abusing years to the slowly-realized truth that I didn't like uptight fine-dining places that much. I switched to working full-time at the airport job. It was a fun place to work and I could actually talk with my customers without them getting offended when I asked them how they were doing. It was definitely a big change of pace and I welcomed it. I was getting tired of dealing with entitled guests, 5am closing time, partying until 7am (Yes, South Beach hours) and going to work hungover to do it over again. Ahh, the younger, invincible days.

But, sadly, I was starting to outgrow them.

### A Quick Moment to Let One Off

Customers say and do a lot of stupid and offensive things, but there is one thing that really gets under my skin that most customers don't even realize is insulting. They ask "So, what else do you do besides bartending or serving?"

Sure, it sounds like an innocent question to most but what else do I do besides this?! Think about what you're implying! That question implies that the job I'm doing is not a "real" job. For most us, this isn't something we just do on the side, it *is our job*. I feel like society as a whole has been programmed to look at any job that doesn't require a degree as not a "real" job. There's also degree holders who do this job vs what they graduate for. Do you not know there's bartenders and waiters that make over 100k a year without having to pay back college loans? Oh man, don't get me started on society.

But please, think before you ask us a personal question and whether or not you'd ask a suit-type the same question. And for the record I do a shit load of things beside bartender and wait, like writing these 15 sentences for this book I wrote. I'll cut this semi rant short because my shows coming up.

We're professionals, too. Treat us that way.

**Fred *Fantastic* Flashback: How You View An Egg**

This celebrity who used to be one of the hosts for the TV show The View (definitely one of the fiery ones) came in to the restaurant I was serving in. She came for breakfast and ordered her eggs a certain way and apparently received them a different way. Man! She threw the biggest fit ever! She was like "Eew this is disgusting. Oh my God. What is this is?'". Turns out her eggs were over-easy vs over-medium. I think the kitchen messed up, but shit happens.

I go into my good-server mode, trying to resolve the issue and said "I'm sorry let us go make you another one". She was still like "Oh my goodness, what type of place is this?!" My inner voice is like: Why is she being so loud?! My pancakes I ordered were getting cold! By the way, we used to get breakfast before or after the initial morning rush and there was a Jamaican chef (what up Jermaine), who made the best pancakes I have ever had. They would put you to sleep (true story, bro). Now, this is like at 7am or something, and I am not a morning person and I get especially grumpy when I'm hungry. After she was still crying about it, I told her "Look Miss, do you want us to make you another one or do you wanna still be dramatic about it?" What can I say, I was hangry. She paused and gave me this look like, did he just?! and then demanded the manager. I got him and let him handle her.

My manager at the time was pretty cool and fought for the employees. After the manager gave the whole blah blah sorry about this, about that, it's on us and all the usual routine to Ms. View, I told him what happened. I went on break and had pancakes, Pancakes. (RIP Charlie Murphy).

Well, you can guess how much my tips was.

I, like a lot of people in this industry, will gladly sacrifice some tips to put someone in their place or call them out when it's called for. It's worth it sometimes. We're servers, not servants, people!

**Side Flashback:** One hectic shift at the airport restaurant, we were severely understaffed with only 2 out of the usual 6 servers, 1 chef and a manager who was losing his shit. Every table was full and food took an average of 45-50 mins. Just a shit show (it happens).

Cuba Gooding Jr. came and sat in my section. Despite everything going around and all the tables around him bitching (rightfully so, for once), he just sat there, cool as ice. Unfazed and very chill. You

KNOW I made sure his food came out on time, even with everything else on fire. I don't know if that's some acting technique but he seemed like a genuine dude. I'll always remember that about him and, hey, the tip wasn't bad either.

## Chapter 7

## My Journey Part 6: Fly high or crash and burn?

The bar and restaurant at the airport closed at 9pm at the latest, unless there was an unusually long delay or something of that nature. Ahhh, I was finally living during normal human hours. On top of the easy hours, I was also in the same county as my house than the hotel so my commute was way shorter. Working at an airport bar is much like any other bar, but there are a couple additions to the customer-type:

> 1. **The customers you could easily tell were afraid to fly**. I'd usually recommend some strong "medicine" from the bar mixed with soda, juice, or even straight-up sometimes and they'd gladly order.
>
> 2. **The customers who were so paranoid about missing their flight they would panic about when the food was coming out.** A few of them would even leave before the food made it out to them. Understand where they're coming from. I would usually tell them one of my cheesy but mostly effective (Don't

ask me how, I'm charming AF) jokes from my arsenal, like: "Look, worst case you miss the flight but I'd still have that bottle of Jameson sitting there at my bar" or some shit like that. Most would laugh and relax a little, some would give me the blank stare. Keeping your shots right?

There was another crazy aspect of the airport bar: A lot of your customers are on the same schedule, more or less, because they're there for the same flights. They all come at you at once, want to order at once, and then check out all at ones. It's just like big waves in long intervals. The prices at the airports are expensive but, hey, we don't make the prices.

So YOU, Mr/Mrs Pushy Customer who always complains about the prices, we know they're expensive but there's nothing we can do about it. Go complain to the owner, not us bartenders. I'll even give you the company email or customer service number. I got you... just don't shoot the messenger. Or they'll tell me that they a flight to catch.

That's crazy right? I thought they just came to the airport to eat and chat with me not fly. Let's use that not-so-common thing called common sense and courtesy.

You wouldn't believe the things certain guests would tell you on a daily. Everything from they are thinking about getting a divorce to what drugs they used to do when they were younger (or are currently on).

The bar, for the most part, was a judgment-free zone. I'm always open to talking with customer and hearing them out. I've gotten everything from numbers from females to job offers from the customer. The bar is the big girl and big boy section. While the table were kids and adult sections. The topic that can be had at a bar is way different most of the time from what is or can be said at table. Good advice (key to life), debatable advice (never get married) and bad advice (customers always right & watch Transformers 3).

I always loved working at a fun environment where I can engage with customers without worrying about offending a customer (loosen up).

By now, you're probably not surprised to hear that I was getting the itch to change jobs again. But this time, I wanted to move back to my birthplace, a tiny town called New York City, permanently. I had always gone back and forth to NY but the last time I had visited, I wanted to stay. The time was ripe, too, because the food and beverage department at this airport had a union, meaning there was a bid for schedules/shifts and the particular bars/restaurants you could choose from. The bid system was based on seniority and even though I started out lucky and liked where and when I was working, I could easily get demoted to a shitty shift at a shitty location if a more-senior employee wanted my spot. I was definitely at risk of being transferred to one of those ol' shitty satellite bars with stale frozen sandwiches that people begrudgingly ordered because they already passed a million choices on their long trek to a shitty airline like Spirit (yes offense. Let's be real.).

I was working with 4 older ladies that looked like they open the airport when James Brown was still screaming please please please and who gambles at the casino with their Social Security checks only playing the nickel slots. They were cool, I mean I felt like the 5th hidden member of the golden girls, just younger and not as adorable, I was the new guy and youngster. That meant I had no seniority, age or time wise on the job. Fast forward a few weeks, I go on a "roundtrip" home in NYC and accidentally didn't come back. Had my reason but the details are insignificant to this book. I wonder what happened to that shift....

**Professional Reviewers**

Reviews on Yelp or whatnot can be helpful to both businesses and customers but some people really don't understand how the scales and ratings are to be used. They will go to eat, receive impeccable service and delicious food and then mark it down from 5 stars to 1, because the place ran out of one item on the menu. Umm… what?! You're either an idiot or an attention-seeking drama whore (and I mean that for both guys and ladies, so chill).

I mean, c'mon guys, be reasonable. Your stupid reasoning is hurting the business because you can't understand what is and isn't out of our control or the fact that we're human and make mistakes. You can't dock us 3 stars because we got one thing out of a dozen wrong. Don't be dumbasses.

Also, it would be really nice if while leaving a positive review if you included the name of your server or bartender. We appreciate the kind reviews for the establishment, but it would be a feel-good boost for us to know how you appreciated our service. Some of you do tell us directly, or indirectly through a good tip, and we appreciate that as well. Some of you do tell us directly and then leave a crappy tip, but anywho... there's something extra when the compliments are written down. But for whatever power-hungry or drama-driven reason, people are more in a rush to write negative reviews than positive ones. If you click on these people's profiles, you'll see a history of bad reviews, coincidence? Don't be like that. If the staff provided great service, tell our manager or post a good review with their name, please. If you're inclined to write a bad review, first ask yourself if you're a making a fair overall assessment on your rating or just an emotional one that's strictly one sided avoiding the good. The only time that answer shouldn't be yes is if you received bad service or bad food *on numerous occasions*.

Again, don't be an unforgiving dumbass.

### Moment with a F&B battle-tested vet:

**Kavita/Server, NY**

**Best thing about the industry?**

One of the perks of being a server is you get to meet

some amazing people and get a new insight or perspective from around the world, which helps you to improve your outlook of the world.

### An industry story you would like to share?

A crazy encounter I've had with a guest was ... the restaurant had two floors so the bar was downstairs and I was serving upstairs. A woman had me walk up and down 5 different times to taste the different options of wine we had, and then she decided to choose water to drink. So then I said "Are you serious?" and she wanted to complain that I was being disrespectful and rude! Long story short, "do unto others as you would your self" – The Bible

# Chapter 8

Let's take another break to honor the customers who didn't quite make the first list of those we love to serve. But this time, I'm not going to just make fun of them. Instead, I'm going to offer some helpful advice on what not to do as a customer. So get your No. 2 pencils ready to take notes.

**Types of Customers We "Love" to Serve: Honorable Mentions**

1. **The refill type:** They usually drink their soft drinks as fast as a guy who realized they left their phone next to their girl. When it's slow, that's no problem but when a server is busy and every 2 mins you're flagging them down for another refill, then yeah, control yourself. Plus, you're slowing us down, and then you like to bitch about slow service. Stuff right here is a contributor of that.

2. **The face blind type:** A customer that's always flagging another server for something and never know what their own server looks

like. Which is sort of disrespectful if you think about it. I mean c'mon, as your server I'm the shit.

### **Flashback**

Customer: Can you tell our server to put another side order

Me: Sure, what's your server name?

Customer: We don't remember

Me: That's ok, what did they look like?

Customer: Don't remember

Me: Male or Female? Tall or short?

Customer: Not sure

Me: (Inner voice: Shit! Did an animal serve you? Were you even served here?) I'll be back.

**3. The come in at closing type:** Seriously, where's the camera? This gotta be a prank. Especially if you've been here before. Give me your work address right now and let me show up at your job when you're trying to leave from a long day of work. What? You're only supposed to be there from 9-5? Too bad.

How does that sound? What you think we're not human too? As a matter of fact, this might be on my personal top 5 Dead or Alive list of things that annoy me about the industry.

**4. The "I don't look before I ask" type:** It's called a menu.

### Flashback

Customer: Hey do guys serve soup?

Server: Yep, right there on the menu where it says soup

(Happens more often then you think)

**5. The "Make the drinks strong and I'll tip you good" type:** LIES LIES LIES. They usually ask you to make the drink strong with a promise of a (subjective) high tip and then they tip under 10 percent. I usually make the drink the same or ask them to order a double shot. You have a better chance of finding a McDonalds with a working ice cream machine than getting a good tip from them.

**6. The accountant type:** Argue about every penny, nickel, tax & etc. They usually think that the server/bartender own the place and made the price.

## Habits that customers should stop:

1. Ignoring ALL the clean tables and sitting at the ONE dirty table. To make matters worse, you're going to complain that the table's dirty. NO SHIT. Tell us more.

2. Just asking for a liquor without specifying what type.

Guest: Give me a beer.

Bartender: Here you go.

Guest: This wasn't the beer I wanted.

Bartender: No? You said give you a beer, so I just spun the roulette and pick the beer the arrow pointed to.

3. Ask for our opinion about food or drinks when you weren't planning on taking it. And when we don't recommend an item, you order it and hate it, guess what? That's right, we are judging you, that's right JUD-GING YY-OOOUUU (internally of course).

I think internet call them Askhole. We're somewhere in the back, making fun of your stupidity. No for real, I'm actually smiling as I write this. I'm getting a kick out of it, at your expense. But seriously, just go with your first choice and stop wasting your time or the rest of YOUR table's time, I'm pretty sure they are hungry.

4. Calling out random drinks to sound cool or to try and one up the bartender. No, we don't know what a flying taco drink is that came out in a shitty bar somewhere in Wyoming (no offense Wyoming). There are so many drinks being created by different bars and club every year, we don't know them all. Stop making shit up, too.

5. We don't care that you can get the same drink cheaper back home at "Fort Who Gives A Shit". We, the bartenders and servers, do not make the prices (I can't say this enough). If we did, we would be on the other side of the bar drinking with you. Now you're holding up the line of 40 people behind you. Order or take this email and message corporate. NEXT!

6. Stop EXAGGERATING your food wait time. You literally ordered your WELL DONE steak 10 mins ago. You have a tendency to embellish the wait time to our manager. Understand certain foods take longer to cook and also you're not the only one getting food in the restaurant.

If you do this to me, understand two things: First, I don't give a shit once you start becoming unreasonable and second, I will show you the ticket time at the risk of me being petty and not getting a tipped. Now, with that being said, if it really did take long, my bad (but really, point the finger at the cook) and I'll handle that.

7. Read the situation. If I'm holding 20.5 dishes in my hands and you see me sprinting because of how crazy it's been, NOW wouldn't be the best time to ask me about the menu or tell me your life story. (Love you tho sweetie, only to the females).

8. WATER! Like seriously, you guys waste more water than an Uncle Luke's Spring Break wet T-shirt contest in the 90's (If you know, you know). Stop asking for water if you're not even going to drink it. Plus, I promise you, your server would be a lot faster.

9. If you ordered from the bar and don't plan on ordering again, DON'T go sit at another server's empty table. Stay at the bar or take your ass to THAT corner right there, yup rii-igght there. Don't sit at another server's table, knowing that a server can't make money as long as you're there. You don't care right? Well, this one is for you.

10. Can I smoke in here? Sure, while you're at it, just blow the smoke right at the 7-month-old baby sitting at the table right next to you. Common sense people. Know what estab-

lishment you're at.

11. Don't make up an allergy or imply it if you don't have any. We would have more respect for you if you just said you don't want anything that's been around peanuts. We take those with an allergy very seriously, so don't make it up, which we notice a lot of people are doing these days. Preference vs allergies… there's a big difference. Of course, do let us know if you're really allergic to something because, you know, we kind of want you living & stuff.

Guest: I'm allergic to peanuts, what can I have?

Server: Oh, the salad and the salmon.

Guest: Okay and is the fries cooked around peanuts?

Server: Yes, sir, it is.

Guest: Any that isn't?

Server: No, sir

Guest: Uh, you know what, I'll get the fries.

Server: But sir, it is cooked around peanuts

Guest: It's ok, I can have it.

Server: Ohh, ok (inner voice: You are full of shit)

12. It's ok to admit when you're wrong. Don't order something and then say you didn't when you did. Especially when I wrote it down and a fellow guest is saying the same shit. You are literally slowing down the whole place down. Some places the waiter has to pay for the food or drink you "didn't order". Now eat that 2 for 1 hot dog with a side of shut the fuck up.

13. Speak up! Look, we're not mind reader. Don't say everything is ok and then go tell the manager or Yelp there's an issue with your food towards the end. We can't solve what we don't know. Help us help you. We don't bite (well, some do).

14. Sitting at the table/bar, seeing we are closing up or past closing time, and just getting even more comfortable. Now we think you're just being an asshole. You have finished with everything but are still hanging around asking "Are you guys closing?" What gave it away?

Was it the lights off, the music stopped, or was it you being the only one in the place with everything locked up?

15. Do not put hair in the food and then complain there's hair in attempt to get us to comp your meal. Morals, people, morals.

16. Please don't take our pens. This should've been higher on the list. It's one of our BIGGEST pet peeves. Matter of fact, this applies to all my coworkers, mom, and everyone.

17. It's ok to say hello back. When we say hello or whatever don't look at us stupid or carry on. At least fake acknowledge us, even if you don't mean it. Because the funny thing is, I am comfortable with ignoring you, too. I'm a natural. I can ignore you all night and besides, I want to finish hearing table #30's story about how he fell off the roof trying to hide from his wife because he got caught cheating (true story bro). Some servers and bartenders will be more brash than me to make sure you heard them, forcing you to respond if you don't want all the customers eyes to stay on you.

18. Get mad when we cut you off from any more alcohol. If you get too drunk and kill someone, we will be held responsible. I'm too pretty for jail.

I could literally go on forever with this, but this book isn't supposed to be that long and plus I got shit to do. I'm sure there's a lot that I missed out on. To my fellow servers and bartenders, send me a message for anything I missed at jumpoff19@gmail.com.

## Fred *Fantastic* Flashback: If I had a nickel for every time…

The airport is an international hub, so I got to meet different types of customers. I was serving these 3 international guests, I think they were German if I remember correctly. Very chill and in a festive mood (or maybe I was, whatever). I remember it was a great interaction and they were big drinkers too. After a few hours they closed and left, saying goodbye. I went to the table to pick up the check and tips.

Maaaan, when I got to the table, I saw stacks of coins. Looking like my dad's dresser when I was a kid. It was about $16 worth of coins broken down to quarters, dimes, nickels, and pennies. I was annoyed, especially having to walk with all of that in my pocket, sounding like a high school janitor with his big ring of keys. As the years went on, I noticed this was a thing with a lot first-timers to the U.S. It's almost like they were saying "Let's unload all these American coins before we go on the next sucker we see". It felt like they were playing pranks on us.

If you're one of them, please stop that. Go to a fast food or something.

So anyway after work, I went to the street offering to break dollars bills for all the change I had by the bus stations. I'm joking. I turned all that shit to the managers when I was closing and kept all the dollars bills. Small victory that day. Score- Server: 5 Manager: 308.

# Chapter 9

## My Journey Part 7: King of NY (not really)

New York City! I was home again, and for good this time.

The first job I landed was a room service position for a popular hotel with a well-known restaurant. I was basically someone who delivered food and beverages to a guest's room at the hotel and, at times, fulfilled certain unusual requests (which may or may not be legal. I know NOTHING!). It was a great hotel and a very exciting job but my schedule required me to wake up at 5 in the morning aaannd... I lasted about 3 days. I'm not the morning type.

Anyway, that's the end of that adventure. On to the next!

My next job was at this lounge restaurant in Brooklyn (represent!). It was perfect. They had music, girls, and the money was good. Yeah, yeah I know, sounds familiar, but the club/lounge life was calling me back to it. I had been away from it long enough that I missed it, despite the crazy hours. The clubs/lounges and I had an on and off relationship and this time we decided to try to work things out.

My desire to work with customers also had its ups and downs. Sometimes, I'd switch to barbacking because I needed a break from dealing with the customers and their stupid questions (yeah, I said it! Now what?). If a customer EVEN glanced in my direction, I would just point to the bartender. It was like someone who spoke English pretending to not speak English.

As a barback, you have to be 2-3 steps ahead of everything. You have to get ice, refill garnishes, replace empty bottles, etc—all before the bartender realizes they need it. You had to neutralize problems before anyone noticed, like the secret service (or is that special ops? I dunno, whatever). The point is, you have to take initiative and get things done without getting in anyone's way. And I was good at it, enough so that I had a bit of freedom to roam, get some food or get into other extracurricular activity without my bartender ever missing a beat. And though I followed my own rules of doing my job well but nothing more, the owners still caught on a few months in that I could actually bartend and put me back in the direct line of customers.

That was was semi okay with me by that time.

With the loose atmosphere, lax dress code, the DJ, and the mingling of customers, this lounge was a mix of a bar, club and restaurant. Food and happy hour were before 10 and then it turned into a dancing lounge after with DJs. It was definitely more of a locals' place, which is sometimes easier because the guests and staff get to know each other and even become friends. I don't know why that friendly atmosphere doesn't happen in all places, but I enjoyed providing the locals with a good stress-free experience. It was a good place to work and still fast-paced but not too commercial (music always helps with that). People came to drink and dance and have a good time and that's what they got.

We did have a $5 cover charge at the door for admission Thursdays through Saturdays, minus females who were always free. A lot of people just paid but of course there were some who were crying about $5. $5?! I mean, what do you plan on doing when you get in? Get some water on the rocks and find a corner to creep from?

Now, I'm not saying you gotta drink or pop some Dom Perignon (is that still a thing?) but most places in the city are charging $20 or more. If you can't afford $5, you need to re-prioritize your life. Go home and text your cousin to send you their Netflix account info... and have them send it to jumpoff19@gmail.com while you're at it. There, now you saved yourself (and me) $13. Ironically, some of the ones that complained the hardest were the ones who somehow had plenty of money for lots of drinks but, not surprisingly, didn't tip. Go figure.

The best part about working at this type of establishment (besides flirting with girls, manager "approved" drinking a lax employee dress code) was we didn't have to tolerate bullshit from NO ONE. See, the rules are just a little different for most sports bars, pubs, and lounges. Meaning, if the customer started shit, we just waved at the bouncer and he'd kick you out. Or, we'd do it ourselves. I've stopped fights and tossed people out for harassing girls, or sleeping because they were drunk, or whatever.

My favorite was CUTTING OFF people, especially the ones who ordered a drink and didn't tip. That's a big no-no, the biggest one actually. If any one of you non-tippers ever wonder if your bartenders are ignoring you after that first drink, well, wonder no more because HELL YEAH WE ARE. I love that shit.

I worked with all females behind the bar (yay!), though one of them was a lesbian so I still had competition. She was the best, though, and was a boss when it came to tipping. She would go right up to you and say "Oh I'm sorry, was something wrong with the drinks?" right in front of his girl or potential roomie for the night. The woman with the guy would normally say something like "What, you didn't tip her?" and the guy would end up over-tipping at her insistence or she herself would tip, apologizing for the guy. It would be a long night for the guy and some of them lost their prospects over it... shiddd, some of them lost their prospects *to* my coworker. True story.

My other coworker was even more of a fireball and would even leave the bar to confront guests who didn't tip. She'd get her tip 99% of the time. Moral of the story? Tip your bartenders! If you can't afford it or don't want to, stay your ass home and sip on a six-pack of beer from Walgreens. There's nothing wrong with that but there is something wrong with not tipping. You don't work for smiley faces, so don't expect us to.

Speaking of female employees, (I can't believe I have to say this but apparently it's not obvious to a lot of customers) don't touch or grab them! Naturally, they hate that shit but, naturally, asshole guys do it all the time. If you do, you're asking to get fucked up by a fellow male coworker (like myself) or even by the badass girl herself.

There are boundaries, people.

It's bad enough if you grab one of us guys but you cross the line big time if you touch the girls. Expect to get handled by bouncers and coworkers alike. Aside from the assholes, it was fun to people watch and to predict girls' reactions to the same old lines of "can I buy you a drink?" or "why do you look so sad?" By the way, dudes, that last line never works… it's insulting to the lady. Lines were fed to us bartenders, too, and I enjoyed it when girls flirted with me, even if they were just trying to get a free shot (it worked on me 2/5 times. Hey, I get weak sometimes).

What didn't work on me was the line "I know the owner".

Oh yeah? That's crazy. Soo, you paying with card or cash for that mushroom bacon cheddar burger with mushroom, bacon, cheddar and bun on the side?

### Server or Servant?

Job descriptions don't mean shit to a server/bartender, aka therapist, entertainer, cook, babysitter, comedian, navigator, photographer, host, owner, and fill in the blank. You are required to do whatever you got to do (by the rules or not) and the pressure can get overwhelming. You gotta know how to sort and prioritize your tasks. Some coworkers get emotional under the pressure, so you have to have tough skin for yourself and others. I've seen people walk out during a shift. I've seen servers fight chefs because the chef was being a jerk or the server got their feelings hurt (poor boo boo). It really can be a volatile environment and you can expect to be underappreciated by managers and customers alike. But, we're not here for hugs and gold stars. We're here for the money, right? Wellll, I'll get into that in another Need-to-Know.

Bartenders do get some sort of shine and come across as the more "glamorous" position like, say, a chef, but that is not the case for waiters. Servers are the unsung, shitted on, and most underappreciated heroes. Bartenders are shielded from some scenarios, like crying babies throwing sugar caddies around or big groups of family and friends ordering everything on the side. Don't get me wrong, bartenders have their own unique BS to deal with, but at least they're able to take a shot whenever they want (shiiit, I know I did. True story, unless a current manager is reading this, of course). Bartenders can also have grown-folk conversations for the most part without somebody being offended. But I DARE you, YOU who is working a regular job and don't think our job is tough, to work in our industry for one week and then tell me you still feel the same afterwards.

We do our best to provide the best quality service

with a smile on our face, but we're human too. Too many customers forget that we are servers, not servants, and treat us like they are our superiors. It's wrong and can be infuriating, but it's a reality of customer interactions. We have to suck it up most of the time, which is done more easily when you trash talk and make fun of them in the back. Or utilize mild sarcasm. But, it's also why I always liked to have a second, back-up job that I affectionately refer to as my "fuck you job" because every now and then, you just gotta go off on a customer and it might cost you your job.

Aaaah, the bittersweet release!

## Moment with a F&B battle tested vet:

### Diandra/Bartender, NY

**Best way to describe the industry?**

There isn't one word to sum up the restaurant industry. If one does exist, I would like to be the first one to know.

**Things you wish customer would know?**

That there is such thing as a stupid question.

**What's the best part of the industry?**

Money is the best when you're weeded.

# Chapter 10

**Story Part 8: Familiar Territory**

After a year and some change, I started to get weary of the hours, same DJ mix, and same type of crowd. Sound familiar? Working at a place like that can wear you down mentally. It's like you want to work there, but once you work there for too long, you want to leave. Being a lounge/club, some weeks were busy and some were not so the money wasn't very consistent either. Plus, there was a shift in power and staff so it wasn't the same type of place that it was when I started. I am still to this day friends with the owners but I was ready to move on.

Like I said before, it's a love and hate relationship.

So, I did what I always did: I switched over to my second job. And you guessed it, it was back at an airport. It was a union-type job again but I will give airports one thing: the customer traffic is practically guaranteed in the restaurants and bars because one they get through TSA, we are their only options. Oh, the monopoly.

It was definitely more reliable money than the clubs, even though the hiring process felt like I was applying for the FBI. I got a position at a famous chef's sister branch of a world-renown restaurant up in Harlem. It was a newish (yup, still using that word) restaurant and it was pretty good. I was back to civilian hours, working no earlier than 7a.m. with the morning shift and no later than 10pm on a nightshift. Much better than the 4pm-5am shifts I was doing at the other place.

This airport job was one of the best places in the industry I've worked (maybe ever), as far as enjoying being there (no offense to any other coworkers). Yes, it was corporate (hate them) but the staff was one of the best and so were the managers. The staff and managers that you work with can make it a way better place (orrr ruin it), where you can handle all the madness and silliness that certain customers can exact upon us. I had a lot of instant chemistry with most of the staff, some took a little longer (D!). The atmosphere was fun and chill. Lots of jokes and fun times while still handling our business.

Take note of that: *while still handling our business*. That's very important. The managers here didn't put a microscope up our butt cheeks and managed when they needed to. A bonus was that most of the bartenders and servers were strong on the floor, meaning they knew what they were doing and took care of the customers. Customers loved the staff, especially the L_ _ _ _ _ _ _n Committee (inside joke).

See, when all you crazy and unreasonable customers leave (some while you're still there), your server/bartender make fun of you and joke about your behavior. I know we did, and rightly so. We are grateful for most of our customers but some of you are plain ridiculous.

For example: those who eat 90% of their food and then complain that the food was terrible and you want to return it or speak to the manager. What?? At what point did you realize you didn't like the food? Was it before or after you ate 5 out of 6 wings? And then you expect it to be comp. That ain't how it works. You wouldn't do that shit with deodorant after using 2/3rds of it. F-O-H. I don't know why you think that logic works in this industry.

And stop being so dramatic. If there's a problem, we are on your side and will try to fix. There's no need for the drama.

The place was big and really busy, but my coworkers and I were well-oiled machines. It was a tough job but a great working environment. I stayed there for a few years but had to move on for reasons I don't think need to explain here.

Maybe over some whiskey if you're buying.

### The Great Ones: The 80 percenters

With those long lists of annoying customer types I provided, I bet you think we must hate almost all our customers, but the opposite is actually true. I'd estimate that we really like a good 80% of our customers, it's just waaaay more fun to talk about the douchebags. And if you fall under one of the "customer types" it doesn't mean we don't like you, but if you fall under several categories then you might want to rethink your personality, you 20 percenter.

What matters most is that you are reasonable and treat us like human beings, and most of you do actually do that. I've even served powerful and famous people who were really down to earth, like the Verizon COO (I didn't even find out who he was until 3 margaritas in).

I've had a lot of great times with customers and learned a lot, as well. Some deep conversation about life and business, learning about where they're from. Life advice (wanted and unwanted). Flight hookups and modeling job offers. Taking a picture with foreigners because apparently, I'm exotic to them. Taking shots with (and probably at) some, laughing (for real) with some, and even hanging out with some outside of work (I know, crazy, right?!).

I've genuinely enjoyed these interactions and am really appreciative to the 80 percenters. They are the reason we make it through our shift, especially our regulars who can make our day just by coming in. Seriously, we're thankful for all you 80 percenters. Enough of this sentimental shit, I almost put on some Lionel Richie.

That is all. Next!


**Fred Fantastic Flashback: Off the Coast of Poverty**

Bad rhythm and awkward moves. Air full of the sweet smell of Bengay and Vicks Vaporub, mmm. Plenty of excitement and false expectations. Lots of wandering eyes, stories, laughter, dirty secrets and MILLIONS OF DOLLARS all under one tent.

It was New Year's Eve just an hour ago and I was

on the beach on a private island for the rich. I had just finished my shift catering to ultra-rich and ultra-old party animals and drove me and some co-workers down to the party to join these old fogies in the festivities.

Now, before you jump to any conclusions, we peons were, in fact, invited to the party once our duties were done. Apparently, not everyone got this memo. Not 5 minutes and three drinks in, Captain Moneypants calls out to me, "Fred? What are *you* doing here?" but in a way that made it clear he was actually saying, "How dare you, you peasant/servant/roach, encroach on our greener grass territory."

Ok, I might be exaggerating but that's how he made me feel. Sad, right? I bet you're feeling sorry my tender little heart right now. Well, don't be, because I just held up my drink to him and said, "Me? I'm enjoying a drink. Same. As. You." He looked at me, a bit in shock that I talked to a member like that, and before he could scold me, I saluted him with my drink and walked away.

Man, it felt good.

# Chapter 11

**My Fellow Industry Warriors**

I gotta give a lot of love and support to all the soldiers in the industry: the waiters, bartenders, bussers, barbacks, hosts, cooks, food runners, and the rest. We go to war with the masses every day and I know you guys don't get enough credit for what we do. I've been in the trenches with you through the ups and downs, and we keep pushing through. Whether you're doing this job temporarily or are making a career of it, don't let the stress affect your overall sanity. Don't let people box you in a label or belittle what you do because they just don't understand. I've seen firsthand how incredible a lot of you are and know how discouraging it can be a lot of times. I know how it feels to not know what might happen next or to deal with the high amount of pressure that comes with this field.

Hang in there, dust it off, and stay positive. Stay armed with our weapons of sarcasm, coffee, and you know what else. You may not hear it enough from managers or customers, so I'll say it for them: We appreciate all you sons of guns!

**My Journey Part 9: Check, Please!**

In the years that followed, I worked at 1 lounge, 1 sports bar, and 3 restaurants. All three restaurant jobs were seasonal, including the private island I mentioned in the last flashback. They are all too recent at the time of writing this book and, well, I don't feel like writing about them. It's more of the same shit for the most part, anyway as far my time in the industry. I've been doing more and more stuff that's actually leading me away from the industry. I'll miss it in a lot of ways but at the same time, I want to leave it forever and never look back.

You're probably wondering why I stayed so long working in a position where I was looked down on and talked down to, but you know what, it's a lot like all those New Year's resolutions that were made that night with the old, pompous guy on the beach. An event happens, like the New Year rolling in, where you get all amped up and decide things are going to be different from here-on. You resolve you're not gonna take no bull from nobody anymore. You salute jerks with your middle finger for the first few days and then... and then... 362 days later you're still working the same job and wearing the same fat-pants.

And you know why you're still wearing those fat-pants? Because you *like* donuts, even though they're bad for you. And I *liked* being a server and a bartender. No two days were the same. I met a lot of different people, co-workers and customers alike. Some I became friends with, some I became *very* close "friends" with and the networking also led to some cool job offers.

You do also get some very weird offers, but you're not ready to hear those yet. The point is, I met cool people like me, crazy people (also like me), future bosses, future spouses... and exes (don't judge me).

Jobs in this industry may be a means to an end for some people or for others, like me, it provides the flexible schedule they need to pursue their passions in the creative fields. Still for others, it's for survival or for a life-long career. The wide range of opportunities within this unique industry helps meet the needs of people of all ages and backgrounds.

I believe the life skills acquired from this field can be used in any other job: being able to stay calm and perform under pressure, prioritizing important tasks, staying organized, a sharp memory (the daily special, not to mention the entire menu, plus who ordered what, and so on), and perhaps most importantly, how to interact with people (the good and the bad). I could go on and on... SO I WILL.

We in this industry are the best at adapting to any situation and thinking on our feet in a work setting. You'd be surprised at how many times the food and drinks you enjoyed were a result of us improvising to make sure you got what you want, not knowing the figurative fires that had to be put out in the back (like a broken grill or running on foot to next door for ice). We are sharp and mentally tough—you have to be to last any significant time in this industry... or crazy. We are good listeners and we could probably outdrink most people (alright alright, that last skill might not be of use in other fields, but bring it on!). Too many people don't consider this a "job" and think anyone can do it but, trust me, many of you wouldn't make it a week in this industry.

I'm going to leave the industry within the next year and thought this was the perfect time to write this memoir of sorts. I thought it'd be good to give a voice to those who work in the backdrop of so many people's lives and to give outsiders a peek into our world. I hope I accomplished that.

So next time you go out, be sure to tip your bartender or server. And be sure to relax and interact with us. We're here to make you feel welcome. Oh, and don't be an asshole.

Cheers!

# Acknowledgments

I would first like to thank Giovanni, the first guy to hire me with my fake-ass resume. Everything started there at your restaurant and I was able to get some real experience that enabled me to move up in the industry. My best friend 1A, Jay for driving me around in the beginning, willingly and unwillingly, to all my interviews and for being my ride at random times in the morning, especially in the earlier club days. Mom, for not asking too many questions when I walked into the house at 7am, smelling like club smoke and cheap perfume, and headed straight to my bedroom to die until I was revived in the afternoon. Besides all that, you're my mom and you made me. Love you. Dad, for also picking me up late at times and for, you know, being my pops. AJ and Bernard BFFs, I mean bros 1B & 1C, for the encouragement during the writing of this book, even though they had different ways of showing it. My siblings Lina, Roger, Barbara, David, and especially my youngest brother, Emmanuel, for always backing me up. Love ya'll. My niece, newer niece & newish, Cherish, Zoey & Isabella. Amy for supporting my idea and for being there. My business partner and close friend, Edwin. Mirah, for indirectly helping with the process. Uncle J, who I'm pretty sure

I got some writing blood from. And Kobe Bryant, just 'cause.

I'd also like to thank all my cool and dope ex/current coworkers over the years for making my work experiences fun and memorable, especially the ones that turned out to be some of my closes friends: Diandra, Dijbril, Simantini (I'm sure I spelled it right), Kevon, Shawnee… man, I could go on and on… Richard aka Gunna Gatsby, Jeff, Angie, Joey, Garth, Kendrick, Jasmine, Jerry, Summer, Rachel, Ashley, Britteny, Amory, Daisy Michael (newish) and so on. Too many to name. I also had some great managers and supervisors that I learned a lot from: Wesley, Harold, Jeff, Whitney, Rae, Dennis, Blake, Daphne, and Manny, for starters. Shout out to "The Boys" in my group chat: John, Fab, and Jhemz. Also to the baristas that kept me going and the MTA drivers that arrived on time. Okay, I'm getting carried away at this point and I might end up thanking everybody I've ever made eye contact with. To wrap it up, I thank all the customers who indirectly paid my bills through the years and gave me the material to write this book. Anybody else I missed, my bad.

www.ingramcontent.com/pod-product-compliance
Lightning Source LLC
Chambersburg PA
CBHW022117090426
42743CB00008B/888